A

MW00460414

# *Smiling Through The Chaos of*

# *Wedding Planning*

A part of "The Smiling Series"

## By Amanda Dawn Hudes

# INTRODUCTION

Are you smiling? If you are sitting there, stressed, unsure of what to do next and anxious about all of this wedding planning to be done, I hope that I have you smiling by the end of this book, feeling more prepared, excited, and at ease.

So why I did write this book? For you. There are wedding planning books out there, sure, but I wanted to write something that really spoke to each of you, really gave you the insider info, not just the generalized TO DO list. I wanted to offer you information without requiring you to read a 500 page book. You're already so busy that the last thing I want to do is to add another action item to your list! Read a chapter at a time if that makes your life easier. This book was written to help you, so no pressure comes with it.

Whether you're someone who plans on hiring a Planner and you want to know what he or she is actually referring to when discussing your wedding options, or if you're someone planning your own wedding, I hope that this book helps you feel more comfortable with the idea of wedding planning.

And I wanted to make sure this book was different, in tone and with a voice that allows answers to questions that you may not feel comfortable asking your Wedding Planner or the vendors you hire. I'm a pretty open person, but I understand the feeling of, "Am I asking too many questions?" when I'm speaking to someone in a profession vastly different from my own. I get it. The feeling of, "Should I be asking this? How do I ask this without feeling like I should know it? I've already asked 2 questions about this topic so now I'm just becoming too much and I don't want to be seen that way" can add anxiety to the process, and I want to focus on helping you relieve some of that anxiety. I hope you feel comfortable asking questions, but it's okay to prefer reading more about the topic and then asking a few follow up questions.

Nothing can replace having someone there to work with, someone who is "your person" while preparing for one of the most memorable days of your lives. "Your person" is there to help you enjoy the process and not worry about the stresses that can occur while planning. "Your person" is there to bounce ideas off of while still being able to maintain your friendships without discussing the wedding during every conversation, and allowing them to be in awe of the beauty that day. So, I do recommend hiring a Wedding Planner or Coordinator. This book will help you plan and understand your options, but it's not meant to replace a Planner. Having someone there to talk to about issues that may come up, having someone to take care of the negotiations and contract reviews, and having someone who is happy to speak with you about all the many pieces that go into this day is irreplaceable.

I'm not going to talk about registries or honeymoons in this book, and I'm not going to get into the details that I would when working on a personal level with you because, with everything in life, I am someone who believes there is no "one size fits all," I AM going to talk to you about the main points in modern-day wedding planning to creating a lower stress environment for the two of you to start your marriage off right and have a beautiful, magical day.

So let's get to it! ☺

# Table of Contents

# RELATIONSHIPS

# THE TWO OF YOU

None of this means anything without a solid relationship.

It is so easy to get caught up in the decision-making of wedding planning that you'll easily find yourself talking about the wedding every time you're together.

"Sorry, what's your name again?"

Yes, that's a bit dramatic, but by the time the wedding occurs, you'll stand there looking at each other the next day like, "Shoot…what do we talk about now?" And of course that's the last thing you want to happen when you marry your bestie.

Okay, now that I've probably scared you a little bit (Sorry!), I want to reiterate this point: make each other the priority. I recommend choosing one of the options below to follow during this process:

1) Choose one day/night a week to discuss all the points your Wedding Planner has brought up over the past week to review or decide on. And don't forget to tell your Planner if

you decide to do this so they aren't wondering why they aren't hearing back from you! If you aren't working with a Planner, discuss a few points on your list (not more than 5 or it will feel overwhelming).

or

2) Chat about a couple of discussion points each day, but commit to speaking about it for 15-20 minutes and then tabling it for the next day if no decision has been made. If there is a decision during that time, fantastic! Let your Planner know the answer to the question they asked and inform them that you will answer the others in the next few days.

Planning your wedding will be a few months or years of your life together, so whenever you get in an argument over any part of it, from the color scheme to the number of bridesmaids there should be, remind yourself of that.

It's totally a personal decision, but I also recommend NOT talking about everything, like hair and makeup. Though some men want to discuss hair and makeup, and some may want to hire stylists for themselves too, the majority will not. Leave those fun decisions to your time working with your Planner and/or your family and friends!

Another challenge that can occur is when family members get involved in the decision-making and it starts to feel less like the two of you being partners making the decisions and more like one of you is being railroaded into certain decisions.

***You're a team.***

Whenever you're not sure what to do, say to yourself, "We're a team. We're partners, and we are in this together." Having that mentality will lead to an even stronger foundation in your marriage. And marriage is about compromise and communication!

What is really important to your partner? Can you give a little? For example, I have a client who often jokes about wanting things a certain way for her wedding. But when it came down to deciding the rehearsal dinner, she decided that even though she'd prefer a smaller group, her soon to be mother-in-law was more important to her, and if she wanted a big dinner, that was totally fine.

*What really matters?*

*If you do get into a disagreement, always bring it back to, "I LOVE YOU!"*

Write a list of what you love about your partner and keep it with your wedding planning files, right on the top of that puppy. You can even add a photo of the two of you.

*Remember what matters, your love and commitment.*

## **Start here:**

I love so much about you. I love your:

| PARTNER 1 | PARTNER 2 |
|---|---|
|  |  |
|  |  |
|  |  |
|  |  |
|  |  |
|  |  |
|  |  |
|  |  |
|  |  |

What I love about US:

| PARTNER 1 | PARTNER 2 |
|---|---|
|  |  |
|  |  |
|  |  |
|  |  |
|  |  |
|  |  |
|  |  |
|  |  |

# WHO TO INCLUDE IN YOUR MAGIC

---

Trust your gut. You have an intuition for a reason. I used to push my strong intuition away, wondering if it were a type of judgement, but a few years ago I decided to listen. And when I say listen, I mean really listen.

It can be scary and difficult to explain to others, but think about this. Babies and dogs either want to go near someone or they want to stay far away. They get a feeling about a person from their energy, and without getting too much into Reiki and other energy healing and movement, think about the way you feel around people. You can close your eyes and know how you feel around someone because it doesn't have anything to do with looks; it's all energy.

When I leave a meeting or a phone call with someone, I think about how the conversation or interaction made me FEEL. Do I feel excited to work together after speaking with them? Do I feel like I could build a working relationship with them?

When I work with clients who know they can rely on me, who place their trust in me and speak with me candidly about challenges in their life, who understand my purpose for them, magic truly happens. When I work with vendors who are passionate about helping others by using their gift and are trustworthy, reliable and honest individuals, relationships grow, and great teams form organically.

Surround yourself with those who you feel you can depend on, those who understand your vision, and those who deeply care about creating the most wonderful experience for you possible.

Having guests and vendors at your wedding who just radiate love and support will create an atmosphere like no other.

# THE DECISIONS

# WEDDING STYLE

## What kind of style do you want to have at your wedding?

Some will say that you should marry (yes, pun intended) the style of your wedding to your personal style. That's not my opinion. And there's really no right answer when it comes to this. While I think it is *easier* to make decisions on décor and style when you're naturally attracted to them, it can be super fun to have that day be really different too!

I worked with a couple who is very athletic and into sports, not a ton of glitz and glamour, but when they got married, the bride wanted SPARKLE! From the dress to the cake topper, wherever she could have sparkle and glitter added, that's what she wanted. She was a princess for the day, and she loved it.

On the other end of the spectrum, I planned another wedding for a couple who really enjoyed dressing up and throwing a great party, but for this special day, they wanted a more intimate affair. The guest list was less than 100 people. The floral arrangements were unique yet simple. The dress and headpiece were fashion-forward with an elegance, the suit was classic, and they felt great. They wanted the focus to be on the ceremony verbiage, on the love, and on the people. This was exemplified even further when they chose to acknowledge every attendee at their wedding during their reception speech.

Your wedding style is the first decision you'll need to make, and it is key in setting the tone for the entire day.

**Based on the style you'd like, you can delve even deeper by deciding the level of formality.**

Below you'll find the standard options of formality for your wedding. I want to start out, however, by saying that you can create your own level of formality. For instance, you can have a super fancy reception held in an open venue location (think beams and the bare minimum) and then have it filled with formal tables and chairs, a super cool patterned dance floor and lighting that will make you feel like you're in a NYC club.

*You want this to feel like your wedding, so think about who you are, what you love, and what kind of feeling you want in that space.*

Hiring a band usually implies a formality of "Black Tie" vs. a DJ hire as a more casual affair. But you can hire a band for a casual affair if the tone of the group makes sense for your wedding style! And every DJ has such a different feeling, so if you choose one that has a more formal approach, why not?

*Ricky Restiano Photography*

Having an actual level of formality to add to the verbiage of your invitation will allow your guests to understand the tone and environment before your special day. If you want a very formal affair, I definitely recommend letting your guests know in advance.

The options of formality:

- White tie
- Black tie
- Black Tie Optional or Preferred
- Semi-Formal / Dressy Casual
- Casual
- Destination

## WHITE TIE

White Tie means formal in every sense of the word. It's definitely not common practice to have a White Tie wedding, but if you want to be super unique and fancy, go for it! What fun! But what's to be expected with White Tie? Women are expected to wear formal floor-length evening gowns with jewels and accessories to match. Men are required to wear a tuxedo with tails, a formal white shirt, a vest and bow tie, gloves and formal shoes. The downside to this request is that this can be quite expensive for your guests just for the attire, so it's best to consider whether that would be feasible for most of your invitees. It will also be quite expensive for you as well, so if you have the financial ability and would love the fanciest of the fancy, this is your once-in-a-lifetime chance to go big.

## BLACK TIE, AND OPTIONS

Black Tie creates the expectation of formal but without the required tails for the men and floor-length gowns for the women. You'll still find many women in long gowns, but they also have the option of a shorter dress in a rich fabric and color. Men wear white formal shirts and tuxes. With Black Tie, you are saying to your guests, "Dress up because you're in for a Saturday night of your lives! From enjoying top shelf liquor and a multicourse dinner, to white glove service, a live band, and a venue that will make you swoon, come prepared for an amazing evening." And how are you telling them this? Oh, with a formal invitation suite of course. I would also recommend hand calligraphy for this invitation style.

Adding "Optional" or "Preferred" to the request for Black Tie allows you to host a very formal event without excluding guests who cannot afford a tuxedo or gown. Some couples also choose to add "Optional" or "Preferred" to the formality listed on their invitation simply because they want the attire to be formal even if they don't plan on creating an extravagant atmosphere.

The word "Optional" allows your guests to wear dark formal suits rather than tuxes and less formal dresses if preferred. Men can still wear tuxedos and women gowns, but they aren't expected to do so. The men can also opt for a long black tie rather than a bowtie.

Adding "Preferred" rather than "Optional" implies that you would like everyone to dress in a formal manner if possible. The only negative about adding either of these words to "Black Tie" is that you will see many variations of what formal means to different people. Thus, if you want a unified look, it's much more difficult when you add "Preferred" or "Optional." Having "Black Tie" or "Semi-Formal" are much easier to understand when it comes to the expectations of attire for the wedding.

## SEMI-FORMAL / DRESSY CASUAL

Semi-formal or Dressy Casual weddings can take place at any time of the day.

Let's say you've always wanted a Saturday night wedding, but you honestly don't have a formal bone in your body, don't worry because you can still have a Saturday night wedding! Just because you have your wedding on a Saturday night doesn't require you to have a formal wedding. The fabric choices and color scheme should make sense for evening, but the actual décor style doesn't have to be elaborate. If you choose "Semi-formal" or "Dressy Casual," you're telling your guests that wearing formal gowns and tuxedos would be inappropriate in this setting; think a nice dress or jumpsuit and a suit. I personally think "Dressy Casual" is contradictory and a bit confusing, so I do not recommend using this phrase on your invitations; I would opt for Semi-Formal.

## CASUAL

Casual weddings have a more laid-back feel when it comes to dress, colors and overall style. You might want a backyard barbeque affair with women attending in summer dresses and men in khaki pants and a patterned shirt and tie. You want a laid-back feel, and you might even include unique entertainment options like life-size board games or a country band for some fun line dancing! Just don't forget that the two of you still need to stand out, so whether you have a really awesome reception entrance (Ever ride on a horse?) or you wear a crown made of flowers and a dress made of lace, remember that Casual creates a relaxed environment, but the focus is still the two of you!

## DESTINATION

If you're opting for Destination, you're most likely going warm, which means airy fabrics and light colors are a must. Even though you might get sweaty, you still want to look the part, so think design more than heavy accessories, shoes and makeup.

For the women, strapless flowing gowns with beachy hair (slightly pulled back since the wind can pick up on the beach) or a cute 2-piece style are great options. For the men, I'm loving the coordinating linen or khaki suits for evening weddings and button-down short-sleeves with rolled khaki pants for daytime.

Just imagine heels, gowns, and formal tuxes and shoes in sand! Imagine glamorous makeup with 100-degree heat melting it! Exactly. Now stop imagining that and make sure it doesn't happen. If you want a formal and glamorous destination wedding, have it in the evening.

Whatever you choose, make sure it feels like you, like the two of you. When you think of the two of you together, do you think formal, casual, or kind of in between? If you're not sure, start looking at designs – dress designs, invitation proposals, and photography styles, and see what resonates with you. What gets you excited? That will help guide you into which direction you should start. Even if you have a wedding in a Halloween theme, it's still a good idea to stick to the above formality options on the invitation. In this case, you would probably add "Costume" or "Masquerade" to "Black Tie."

The next decision is the venue. If you've decided on a formal affair, renting out a barn just wouldn't fit "the feel," so what makes sense? Sticking to the idea from the start will help the day/night feel cohesive.

# VENUE

---

There are so many venue options to choose from, so I recommend the following:

1) **Decide your "Wedding Style," including Formality.**

2) **Research venues and make a list of your top 10 (or fewer).**

3) **Have your Planner find out the venue's available dates if you know the time of year but aren't set on a specific date, or find out if they have availability on the day you have chosen. You may want to speak about pricing at this time as well, or wait until the sixth step if you aren't on a super tight budget.**

4) **Review your list and place a star next to the venues that make sense for you with regard to availability.**

**Side note:** It's good to ask venues how many weddings they have going on simultaneously so you aren't shocked on the day of when you see another couple and their family and friends.

**Another side note:** Consider the time of year when you think of questions to ask the venues. If you're Jewish and you're getting married around Christmas, most venues will have holiday décor up, so find out what they will have so you aren't shocked or disappointed. I had this occur with a wedding I was doing Month-Of–Coordination for. Unfortunately, I wasn't hired until after they had booked the venue, so when we went to view the hall the month of, my clients were shocked to see a huge Christmas tree in the lobby. They had initially seen the venue during a different season, so they didn't know that the venue decorated that way around the holiday season. Fortunately, I was able to discuss options with the venue and have them add a Menorah into the décor as well so my clients and their guests would feel comfortable.

5) **It's now time for you or your Wedding Planner to make appointments with the venues you starred so you can see them in person and really get a feel for the environment and the people you'll be working with (super important).**

If you are doing the planning yourself, try to get one contact person who you will speak to throughout the process when you make the calls to the venues. The last thing you want is to be given information by one person and then see the venue and find out it's completely out of your price range or not even available anymore. If you speak to one person, you can ask a couple of key questions on the phone that will determine whether you want to see the space in person, and then tell them that you look forward to meeting with them. Remember, everyone you work with is a kind of relationship for the next ___ number of months /years, and you want it to feel comfortable. If you aren't comfortable with the individual but love the venue, depending on the venue, there may be other people you can work with instead. With some, however, you don't have options of alternate staff, so that's something you'll need to decide how important it is to you.

*Ricky Restiano Photography*

*Who you work with for your wedding is about their work AND their work style. This includes every professional you work with for your special day.*

Work style includes personality, efficiency, proactive or reactive approach, organizational skills, and even communication style (i.e. text, email, phone). Their style has to vibe with yours in order for you to have the most pleasant experience possible. For example, I will text with clients sometimes, but I make a point to say in the beginning that I don't text "To Do's" because I like to keep things organized in email and my online calendar. That's just what works best for me, and when I am organized, I do the best job for my clients. If someone is not at all a phone or email person and they only like to text about everything, we aren't going to be the right fit. And that's okay! It's about working with the person / people who make sense for YOU.

*Think about your personal style and what will work best for you so that you are stressing less and enjoying more. There is no right or wrong; it's just what suits YOU.*

It's not about changing people but about appreciating that each of us has unique qualities to offer one another and figuring out who helps you smile through the chaos.

## 6) Time to see the venues!

Before you go, decide what is an absolute MUST. You may be obsessed with chandeliers and say, "I need to feel like I am Cinderella," or want the complete opposite where you don't want a grand ballroom at all but rather a really cool industrial space! Whatever your vibe, go with that and make sure the venue has that "must have" so you can feel like, "Yessss…this is the one!"

When you're at the venue, there are many detailed questions for you or your Planner to ask, but one that you may not consider until you see your great-grandmother trying to find a way to see you in your dress before you walk down the aisle is, "Where is the bridal suite?" If it's upstairs and there are no elevators, you may not be able to have those with disabilities or the elderly visit you in that area before the wedding ceremony. That's not to say, "Don't book the venue!" There are plenty of gorgeous venues with this layout, and it's really just about weighing what is super important to you for your wedding. Again, there is no right or wrong. Just having the facts allows you to make the right decision for YOU.

### *Take a look at all of the rooms.*

You'd hate to realize later on that you have to go back to look at the rooms again because you only viewed the one you THOUGHT you would need when now your list has grown and you'll need their largest available space. Oh, and you never saw the room they will be opening up for the Viennese dessert time! Take pictures if they allow, even if you're told that there are pictures on the website. You want to look back at pictures that come from your personal view so you can really get a feel for the space.

When you're at the reception location, or when you're discussing with your caterer, be sure to speak about table options as well.

## FOYER OR GUEST LOUNGE AREA

- What size and what shape is the Place Card or Escort Card Table?

- Do they have another table for your guestbook? You might need an easel or other specific arrangement instead, but that depends on your wedding décor.

- Do you want lounge furniture for guests to relax or would you prefer a standing room prior to entering the cocktail hour? You might also want to consider the lounge furniture as a part of your wedding reception, along the sides of the room!

## COCKTAIL HOUR

- How many high tops (tall cocktail tables) and how many standard cocktail tables will they have out for you and your guests?

## RECEPTION

- How many guests to a table?

  o Think about the number of guests you plan on having to celebrate the day, as well as considering the guests who know each other. This will be especially important while you're doing the seating arrangements. For example, if you have 100 guests and the tables seat 10 people each, you know that you'll have 10 tables set up, but if 15 of them all know each other and don't know anyone else, it might actually work out better if you had smaller tables so you can split the group up into 2 tables and the other guests into the appropriate tables as well. Or, on the opposite end of the spectrum, you might want long tables that will sit 15-20 each. Seating arrangements can become very complex, so it's best done drawing it out with pencil and easily moving people around. Be sure to ask the venue for a floor plan so you can plan accordingly.

o   Some couples prefer to have all guests at a table know each other so they can just enjoy. Others prefer to mix up the tables a bit to reduce the number of different groups and create one big group instead. It really is your personal preference. The positive to having tables by commonality like "workplace" or "high school friends" is that there is an automatic familiarity and ease in the room. The positive to having tables combined is that your wedding will become a place for all to enjoy together.

o   If you are close to your parents, you will most likely want them at a table nearby yours, and combining the two (or more if there are step parents) families at the table is a wonderful idea to creating an environment of love and welcoming. The exception to this would be in an unfortunate situation of family members not getting along to the point of a possible awkward or uncomfortable atmosphere for all. In that case, I would suggest separating the tables so your day remains pleasant and peaceful.

- Will the two of you sit with everyone, at a Head Table, or at a Sweetheart Table?

  o Deciding to sit with everyone usually occurs if you are a couple who does not like the spotlight. You want to blend in as much as possible and just have a blast with your friends and family.

  o If you decide to sit at a Head Table, you'll be sitting with your wedding party on each side of you, either alternating sexes or having your party on your side (the right side) and his / her party on their side. Be sure to include their dates at the table so their partners aren't feeling awkward or left out. If your wedding party is big, you can also separate the tables, having your party and their dates at one table and his /her party at another table with their dates. Having "wedding party tables" is not required, just an option. They can also sit with the other guests if you feel the personalities or backgrounds would work better.

    ▪ What kind of décor would you like for your Head Table? Chandeliers hanging above, garland with gorgeous flowers draped across, a patterned runner across the table, drapery, marquee letters, overhead greenery or florals, hanging lights strung across the ceiling, the options are endless.

  o If you and/or your fiancé have children, the two of you may choose to sit at a Head Table with your children. I think it's a beautiful way of saying, "WE just got married, combining families and becoming one."

- Tip: Discussing the seating arrangements with the kids beforehand will relieve you of having to speak about it at the wedding, so let everyone know their seats prior to the entrance into the room.

  o If you decide to sit at a Sweetheart Table, it will just be the two of you sitting together. You'll have a view of everyone enjoying themselves, with the band or DJ directly across from you on the other side of the dance floor. This will allow the two of you to have a few minutes to eat your meals, steal a few kisses, and to be the main attraction for everyone to make cute little noises over ("Awww….look at them").

    - What kind of décor would you like at your personal table? If you want to keep to the same floral theme as the guest tables, I suggest keeping to the same colors but changing the size and / or the exact flowers to make your floral décor unique.

- What shape tables do they offer?

  o Some venues only offer oval, some round, some square, really, there are many options and if you're looking for a specific look, this will help determine your venue as well.

  o Knowing the shape, as well as the size, will help you determine which centerpieces will look best.

- What linen options do they provide for the cocktail hour tables and the reception tables? Are there others for an additional cost if you so choose?

- How big is the Cake Table?

<u>If you decide to have your wedding at your home (or a family or friend's home), there are few keys details to remember:</u>

1) Guests will need washrooms. Will the guests be using the house bathrooms or will you be renting portable toilets?

2) If outdoors, will you be renting a tent? Does the house have natural décor such as beautiful floral landscaping?

3) Where are the outlets? Write this number down and provide information to vendors such as the DJ and caterer.

If you plan on having an after party, take the pressure off of the two of you and have your wedding party handle it, or extend the party at the same location for an easy switch. And when I say "same location," I'm referring to a separate bar area at the venue, but it can also mean the same location as everyone will be sleeping, such as a the hotel bar or lounge area.

Creating an entirely separate party post wedding is asking for a lot more work and some disappointment since sometimes people stay and sometimes people go. It should just be a fun "extra" if guests want to continue the fun. This is your time to just RELAX!

You may even want to bring a more comfortable after party outfit, like a cute white mini or a lace jumpsuit! Wear what you will feel comfortable in, but also what you'll be excited to leave the party to go back and celebrate with your partner!

Regarding the extra fee for an after party, you have options with this as well. You can have the first hour be on your tab and then after that everyone is on their own, you can pay for 2 hours of open bar, or you can have everyone just pay for their own. I always think it's nice to pay for something, so people who want to extend their time with you don't feel obligated to have to spend money at your wedding (even though it's technically after your wedding).

# COLOR SCHEME

## I recommend choosing your color scheme AFTER you choose your venue.

But why?

Each venue has a certain look, and that includes patterned rugs, painted walls and specific details that make them special. Imagine you chose the color scheme of pastel blue and pink. You then choose a venue that has a deep red and gold patterned rug all around the dance floor. Your décor is full of pastels and the rug is a deep red and gold. Yea. I can imagine your facial expression and it's probably similar to mine right now. So that's why.

However, there is a caveat! I do think it's a good idea to review color options first and then visit venues with an open mind, keeping note of the colors you are considering using.

My own personal general rule is to choose a pop of color with 2 neutrals, but I go outside of this rule all the time, sometimes choosing 2 pop colors with 2 neutrals. To make a general statement, I don't recommend having more than 4 colors or it can become too wild looking (unless you're having a carnival theme!), but you also want to have a splash of color or it can become too drab looking. When I'm creating color schemes for clients, I utilize my experience in the color and fashion world combined with the vision I get from my clients thoughts and styles to create a customized look that will produce a beautiful atmosphere.

**If you want to try and create your own color scheme, here are a few steps I recommend:**

1) What's your favorite color? Now, I don't mean your favorite color in general, I mean when you look at wedding photos, do you tend to get excited when you see pastels, deep jewel tones, glitter? What are you attracted to?

2) Think about the time of year you want to get married. If you're considering a wedding of deep jewel tones, that might not look right for an outdoor summer wedding. But of course…it's your wedding, so if it makes you happy, go for it!

3) If you're having a wedding party, consider colors that will be flattering for them as well. I know, I know, it's your wedding, but these are also your closest friends and family, and you want them to feel great too. The happier everyone is, the better your wedding day will be for everyone!

Now that you have the style, the formality, the venue, and the color scheme, you can officially announce your engagement with a Save-the-date card and/or personalized website! You can also start looking at invitations.

# INVITATIONS

Between all the paper options (and other materials!), the color schemes, and the choices of fonts, deciding on your invitation and calligraphy can be quite daunting. It all goes back to the style, the first point in this book. Is your wedding going to be a very formal black tie event, a backyard farm setting or somewhere in between?

*Your invitation will set the tone for what your guests are to expect.*

Just picture this. You receive an invitation in the mail to your cousin's wedding. It's wrapped in an 8x8 square pocket folder made of raw silk with a gold foil handwritten script stating your name and address on the envelope. I don't think I need to continue without you already knowing that this wedding is going to be a lavish affair. You wouldn't send such a formal and expensive invitation for a casual barbeque wedding where you want people to dress in cowboy boots and summer dresses. That would be very confusing for everyone.

I have found that the personal budget for invitations varies greatly, so just keep this in mind: the more formal the wedding, usually the more expensive the invitations, the gown (or multiple gowns!), the flowers, and other pieces to the puzzle. Even for casual weddings, when it comes to this part of the wedding planning, people's mouths drop open when they hear how expensive high quality invitations can cost. But again, it all comes down to prioritizing in your budget. Some of you are committed to having amazing invitations, and this part of the planning can be super fun for you!

*Again, think about your color scheme, the formality of your wedding, your overall vision, and creating "a look." That can be achieved with any budget, large or small.*

No matter what your style, there are a few elements that are recommended to be included in all invitations.

The wording should include who is hosting the wedding. This is very personal. The options are many, but the majority of you will include one of the following:

- the bride's parents (or one partner in the case of same-sex weddings)
- the names of both sets of parents
- your names
- your names with your parents names

For example, you can say something like, "Together with their parents, Lisa Evans and James McAffrey invite you to celebrate...."

If you're getting married for the second or third time and you have children, you can say, "Joining two families as one..." or "Together with their families, Lisa Evans and James McAffrey..."

If any parents are deceased and you want to include their name in your invitation, you can certainly do so. Adding "late" before their name(s) is a wonderful way to honor them.

For example, "Lisa Evans, daughter of Dr. Kyle Evans and the late Mrs. Emma Evans, and James McAffrey, son of Mr. Benjamin and Penelope McAffrey, request your presence..."

I know how complicated family situations can be, so I want to be super clear in saying that I don't want the process of deciding on invitations adding any stress to your life when you already have the actual family challenges to get through. Thus, when you have divorced parents who are either single or remarried, you might not be sure how to word your invitation. If you want to include everyone as hosts, you can certainly do so. Keep couples together on one line.

**Example:**

Dr. Kyle Evans and Faith Nom
and Mr. Keith Under and Carly Under
and Mr. Seth Meet and Sara Meet
request your presence at the wedding of their children
Neema Under and Wyatt Meet

I'm more of a modern style individual than traditional, so I tend to prefer keeping everyone's names separate rather than adding the traditional language of the man's name only, but that's my personal opinion. If you want to have the man's name only, that completely works as well!

**Traditional example:**

Mr. and Mrs. Larry Reif

**My personal preference:**

Mr. Larry Reif and Mrs. Beth Reif
or
Mr. Larry and Mrs. Beth Reif

Again, there is absolutely no set rule that you must follow! This is YOUR wedding. I remember being told that the traditional style was the way I should have my cards addressed for my wedding, but I'm way too much of a feminist to keep the women's names off the envelopes. And when we were introduced as husband and wife, you better believe my first and last name were being mentioned. But that's ME! I'm giving you a piece of me in this book so you can see that there are many ways of doing things when it comes to wedding planning, and the only thing that matters is that YOU ARE HAPPY.

You'll want your names in the largest font so everyone opening the invitation will immediately know who the invitation is for and what they are being invited to celebrate. Formal invitations should include the middle name in addition to first and last names, as well as titles.

After stating the necessary names (Phew – that's done!), invite your guests to celebrate with you by requesting their presence, inviting them to join you in celebrating, or asking them to honor you with their presence. There are many options when it comes to wording, so try a few and see what feels good to you.

Definitely don't forget the date and time!

If the invitation style is formal, every word and number should be written out in full. You can either say "a.m." or "p.m." as well as "in the evening" after the time is stated. For more casual weddings, feel free to use numbers for the time. For example, a formal invitation might read "four o'clock in the evening" while a casual invitation might read "4p.m."

If the reception does not immediately follow the ceremony, write the start times for both so guests can plan accordingly.

Depending on whether you will be having your ceremony and reception in one location or in two, you will either include the one location or you will write the ceremony address first and the reception details second or on a separate card in the invitation suite.

Unless the wedding is being held at a private home, the full address does not need to be added. The name of the venue, along with the city/town and state should suffice. However, if it is being held at a home, make sure to include the address that shows up in a GPS as well. Having guests show up late because they couldn't find the location is the worst. If there is a "Franklin Street" and a "Franklin Rd" in the same town, specify the exact address, even adding a street marker if that helps.

And now here is where the dress code comes into play. Adding "Black Tie" and such is not absolutely necessary if the invitation states it is so in design and obvious expense. But to guarantee clarity, adding the dress code to the bottom of the invitation is an easy way to ensure there is no confusion.

You want to feel that the invitation is "you," so read it aloud a few times, read it to each other, read it to your closest friends and/or family if you want, and then set it down. Once a decision has been finalized, there is no point in reviewing it in your head again and again. It's set. It's perfect.

For more of a "do it yourself" style, you can order from websites like Minted or Zazzle. Depending on the paper and style you choose, it's really a personal opinion of whether the quality is what you're looking for, so having that 100% satisfaction guarantee can set your mind at ease.

Some sites offer great options with coupon code promotions emailed all the time, often times for 50% off! With a variety of paper options, they provide you with the design and personalization without the high cost.

Etsy (love that site!) also has designers who set up individual shops and are available to answer questions about the invitations and other design elements. I love supporting artists, and I thoroughly enjoy pairing different pieces together from such a fun website to create a theme or tone.

I partner with an invitation company, so my clients have a variety of choices at their fingertips (literally). They choose, with or without my guidance, the style they prefer from the website I send them, and then we place the order. But I also contact other designers if I love their designs! Unless they request that I choose everything, I always like to provide my clients with several options. With so many possibilities out there, I am never one to say, "Nope! I only work with one invitation designer/company so if they don't have what you're looking for, well, sorry." This is about YOU and making sure you are happy.

The first thing I do after having the initial consultation with my clients is pull from inspiration and color what mood and feel I'm envisioning for the event. Many times this includes invitation styles and ideas. Having the visuals makes it easier to discuss the vision with invitation and floral designers.

Many companies and designers are happy to provide you with a sample for a small fee before placing a large order. I highly recommend seeing a sample invitation first so you feel good about the quality and design being presented to your guests. I can't tell you how many times the samples have looked so different than they did online. Whether it's the paper weight, the print quality or the colors, viewing it in person will give you a much better idea of whether it's the right choice for your wedding.

If you're deciding between a few and are on a tighter budget, keep in mind that the postage fees will coincide with the larger size, the heavier the paper stock, and the increased number of pieces to the invitation suite.

Regarding postage, I love a good "Love" stamp since you can order several books and still feel comfortable using any remainder post wedding for other mail. I have also recently become obsessed (not literally) with the idea of matching the stamps to the invitations, as some designers are offering.

Calligraphy is a gorgeous way to add formality to your invitations. There are amazing artists who do such beautiful work. I appreciate their skill to the fullest since I joke that I received praise for my handwriting in the 3rd grade so I kept it as is. Yes, I'm being serious. That's how bad it is. And that's why this book is typed. And why I'm so grateful to be living at a time when we so often speak through type.

Computer-generated calligraphy / printing is also a beautiful option for a smaller budget and / or less formal appearance. You won't get a designer's personal style or the raised font, which is really special, but you can get the script design.

Having guests RSVP to you via your wedding website or even to your email address is a cost effective, yet less formal, way to manage the RSVPs. By adding, *"Please RSVP directly on (add your wedding website here) by _____ date"* at the bottom of the invitation, you are advising everyone that you will be managing the responses online rather than using the traditional method of postal mail. You can customize your form online to gain all information you need, including allergy information, which those who have greatly appreciate.

The more traditional, and more formal way of managing RSVP's, is by mailing an RSVP card along with the invitation for the guest to return to you via snail mail. The RSVP card envelope should be self-addressed and stamped so all that is required of the guest is to write their name and check off if they will, or will not, be attending.

Depending on the size of your parties, you also have the option of asking guests if they will be attending different events during your weekend, an example being your rehearsal dinner or your day-after brunch.

In some less formal instances, the caterer will request for your guests to choose their entrée in advance and check one of the options you list on the RSVP card.

If you're providing a Details card, or an Accommodations card, you'll offer information regarding their guest stay at the hotel block (Yes, I highly recommend setting up a hotel block at one or two hotels nearby the venue, depending on the size of your wedding.). You can either provide information regarding transportation to and from the hotel to the wedding on this card or in your letter to be placed inside the Welcome Bag they receive upon arrival to the hotel.

And yes, Welcome Bags are SO appreciated by guests, especially those who have been traveling for hours to be there for your special day. I'm not going to go into the specifics of what I recommend you adding to these bags or to the Bathroom Baskets here since I believe in customizing everything for you. You know your guests, so while I can recommend certain "must have" items, I do think adding that personalized touch is really special. I highly recommend asking the hotel in advance whether they have a charge for passing out your Welcome Bags as guests check in or placing the bags in their rooms in advance as a surprise when they enter their rooms, exhausted from traveling.

# CEREMONY

---

Remember, most people have some nerves going when they're up there in front of so many loved ones, so you aren't alone. If you fumble on your words, just laugh it off because it's about your love, not about your ability to speak perfectly. Everyone is there to support you and your union.

If you are writing your own vows, I very highly recommend having someone read both of your vows before you say them to each other. Now, this is not the case if you are someone who prefers to just speak from the heart, but rather for those of you who want to write out your vows in advance. The reason I recommend having the same person read both is the following:

1) If one person's vows are 5 pages long and the other person's vows are a few sentences long, one or both will most likely feel a bit embarrassed.

2) If one person's vows are almost entirely filled with stories and some humor and the other person's are pouring their heart and soul out to the other person, it might create an awkward atmosphere.

Choose someone you both trust to read them and not say anything more in response than, "Looks great," "I would probably write some more" or other very general feedback. Decide between the two of you what you want to hear from them and let them know in advance.

If you are entering into a marriage with children, either together or from past relationships, including them in your vows is a really special way of honoring them. Depending on the age of the children, you might want to have them say a little speech at your wedding (ceremony or reception) as well.

I have the personal experience of getting married privately in a destination wedding and then having a big ceremony and "party-time reception" with loved ones. I also have the personal experience of getting remarried years later and having an elegant second wedding. The latter included each of our children from our previous marriages. We wanted to make sure they felt super connected as well, so we included them in several areas: the ceremony vows, standing on each side of us, the reception entrance, sitting with us at our Head Table, and even joining in during our first dance once we had a few minutes of dancing as a couple.

***So I get it. I understand Wedding Planning from a personal perspective as well, not just from a Wedding Planner professional perspective.***

Every ceremony is different, even if many of the words are the same. Try to take it all in, taking in the smiling faces as you pass them walking slowly down the aisle, taking in the look on your soon-to-be husband/wife/partner as they see you walking towards them, ready to make your full commitment to them.

Really look at them when you say your vows. As you've heard so many times before, it all goes so quickly, so try to enjoy every moment so you can treasure them for a lifetime.

I love when I hear guests say they were crying during the ceremony because it was so beautiful. Heck, I've gotten teary-eyed for many! Having the honor to view love at its finest is so magnificent.

One suggestion to create a relaxed and elegant atmosphere before your ceremony begins and while your guests are waiting is to have servers hand them a glass of champagne or prosecco, or even sparkling water with lime, as they enter the ceremony location or venue. You can also have glasses set up on a table for guests to take as they enter for a less formal yet still elegant atmosphere.

A special way to allow other friends and family members to take part in your wedding is to request the honor of having them pass out customized ceremony programs to each guest as they enter the seating area, or by placing one on each seat prior to the guest arrivals.

You also have the option of placing programs in a basket for guests to take at their leisure prior to the ceremony.

Design-wise, your ceremony program should have the same style and formality as your invitations and other printed items, such as the menu and escort cards. Regarding content, I advise keeping it simple and personal. To further explain, creating a clean-looking program that allows guests to easily understand the order of the ceremony, as well as the wedding party details, is key. If you include too much verbiage, it can become too overwhelming for guests. You want people sitting down, chatting with other guests, reviewing the program and getting excited to see you walk down the aisle. If you give them a book, they are either going to all have their heads down trying to get through it before the ceremony begins or they won't read it. Adding a personal touch, such as a small blurb about how you two met, adds a cute little touch.

# REHEARSAL

Not everyone has a rehearsal, but if you do decide on one, keep it light and easy. It's really just to make sure the two of you, along with your wedding party and immediate family, feel at ease for the big day, knowing where to walk, the order in which everyone walks, and the coordinated pairs walking down the aisle. If you have a rehearsal, you will probably want to have a rehearsal dinner as well (Don't forget to book this in advance, especially if you have a large guest list!). If you would like to have a big rehearsal dinner, this will also need coordination and planning.

Depending on the location of the wedding ceremony, you may or may not be able to utilize the same space for the rehearsal as your actual wedding. Venues are often times booked up the night before, but not to worry one bit. As long as there is a space to walk, you can really do the rehearsal anywhere, even at the restaurant before eating your meal. Again, it depends on the formality that you want for your rehearsal. Some people want a really formal wedding, but they want the rehearsal and day-after brunch super casual. Or you may want an entire weekend of opulence!

# OFFICIANT

---

*It's not just about what someone says but how they say it.*

In most instances, you'll sit down and have a conversation with your would-be officiant for a discussion about A) what the two of you are looking for in an officiant for your special day, and B) your relationship, so the officiant can learn more about you as individuals and as a couple.

The officiant will also discuss the steps in receiving your marriage license before your big day, so hiring someone with experience is very important.

What, if any, religious aspects do you want for your ceremony? If you do want the ceremony to be religious, how do you want him or her to address the almighty?

Do you want a lengthy ceremony or a quick 15-minute one?

Will you want any loved ones to stand up and read any poems, scriptures, or other meaningful words?

You might also want to include some cultural or traditional aspects to your wedding. If you celebrate Catholicism, will you want to include Mass? If you celebrate Judaism, will you want to circle around one another 7 times during the ceremony or would you prefer to include something more standard like the breaking of the glass?

Some officiants like to add some humor into the ceremony, while others prefer to keep it very by-the-books and serious. It's important to understand their style before hiring them or you may be very disappointed while standing up there at the altar.

Having someone who you feel comfortable with is so important. Your nerves might be a bit shaky with a small or large group watching you get married, so having someone whom you can turn to while they speak words that mean so much to the two of you will really help.

I have seen and heard a few stories that would make you cringe, so one important detail I would advise is to make sure both the Officiant and your musical entertainment are all well versed in the pronunciation of your names before saying them aloud to all of your guests.

"Everyone, we now pronounce them man and wife, Mr. and Mrs. Steinberg!"

Umm…it's "Steemberg." Whoops.

Yes, I'm being totally serious.

# CONTRACTS

---

### HAVE A CONTRACT WITH EVERYONE.

I cannot emphasize this more.

I will literally go back and forth with someone 10 times if I have to in order to make sure the contract protects my client. I advise keeping a folder or binder for contracts, or copies of contracts if you're working with a Planner.

I've been known to create contracts when there isn't one (And no, this is not in my contract, but that's how strongly I feel about making sure my clients are protected). And yes, if surprise could have a sound I have heard it many times over the phone when a vendor says he or she does not have or use a contract and I reply with, "Oh! I can create one if you're open to using one." They always say yes. If they say no, that should be a red flag.

*If they will not have any form of legal documentation stating that they are responsible to perform an act of service or provide something tangible for your special day, I would run far far away.*

Some businesses try to sneak travel fees into contracts as well. I am a huge believer that all fees should be made transparent to the client and the Planner. If a vendor asks for the location and timing of your wedding so they can provide you with an accurate quote, they should also provide you with any additional costs you may incur, such as travel fees, at that time. These additional fees add up, and some can be astronomical, so definitely confirm the total cost before any contract is signed!

In my opinion, signing a contract with someone is saying, "I very much look forward to working with you. This contract will be used to set expectations of service." Though the contract should definitely include all "just in case anything goes wrong" details, I am a big believer that once it's set, there has to be some trust that goes along with it. You are hiring that business because you love their work, you have a rapport with them, and you trust that they are going to help make your wedding day the most amazing day of your life thus far.

Before the contract is even created, decide if you enjoy their presence because they are going to bring that energy to your wedding day.

**Read that over again.**

A bad attitude from the start is going to be a bad attitude at your wedding, and that is definitely not the tone you want on your day. When you hire a Planner, your Planner should also be getting a feel for each vendor and how it would be to work with them. How responsive are they? Do they treat you like a number or like someone they are really excited to work with? What do others have to say about their time working with those vendors? It's very important for me, personally, to work with people who keep me smiling so I can help my clients smile through the chaos!

Ask questions. Especially if you're trying to decide between a few different vendors, asking questions will allow you to learn more about their work and their personality to know who will be a better fit for you. If you work with a Planner, the Planner should know what questions to ask, and when to negotiate as well.

Contracts should be fair for both parties, protecting both sides. For instance, my contract is about 10 pages long, including detailed information so each party is clear of what is expected and what is included. An example of a photographer's contract would be including the number of photos that you should receive, the number of hours they will be photographing your wedding, including start and end times, what is included in the package (ie wedding album, engagement photoshoot, etc.), exactly who will be taking the photos, and other such details. If you're wondering why the "who" is included, it's because there are times a couple will hire a photography business, or other vendor for their wedding, without contracting the specific person they are interested in. They later find out that even though they booked the company, that specific person is already booked for another wedding and they'll be getting someone else that day.

Will the photographer have an Assistant that day or a Second Shooter? Yes, these are different titles and I will explain. An Assistant helps the photographer(s) by carrying supplies and helping to set up shots. The main photographer you hire may bring a second photographer with a similar style but a unique eye. That Second Shooter will capture photos at the same location, such as during the ceremony, as well as in different locations, separating so each be with one partner while preparing for the wedding. This is why questions are so important! It's not just about hiring a photographer anymore.

When I first met my now friend and colleague, Christine Merson, owner of Christine Merson Photography, she mentioned right away that she always includes the option of a Second Shooter and automatically includes one in her higher end packages because she realizes the importance of covering all aspects of weddings. As soon as she said that to me, that elevated her standing in my book because she realizes that having someone else with her, not as an Assistant but as a Second Shooter, will allow the couple to be able to see each other in photos after the wedding during moments they didn't get to see on that day.

That leads me to....

# PHOTOGRAPHY and VIDEOGRAPHY

*Does the photographer you're considering booking have the style you're seeking to create "that feeling?"*

It's really important to know the style of a photographer before hiring them so your expectations correlate with the results.

The first place many of us run to nowadays is social media and a vendor's website, but it's important to realize that a photographer is never going to post a photo they don't think is a good representation of their work. Understandably, they post photos that they want clients and potential clients to see. What about the others? Ask to see a few full galleries from weddings they have shot so you can see how many out of those you love and whether they're what you're looking for. For example, if you're getting married in a city, ask to see albums from city weddings so you can get a good idea of the type of moments they capture. During the "first look," did they capture any close up shots of the couple's emotions or were all very far away? It's very personal! Now, to be fair, they may not

*David Starke Photography*

have taken photos of everything you would because the couple didn't want those captured, but if none of the albums display what you're looking for, it either may not be the right fit or it may be worth a discussion. I wouldn't suggest just sweeping it under the rug and hoping that they shoot those specific moments at your wedding. Like in all relationships, communication is key.

One client, let's call her Neema for privacy sake, saw a friend's wedding photos and thought they looked classic and beautiful, so she decided to book the photographer. She didn't realize that she was seeing a few amazing photos, but the true style of the photographer was very different than she had thought, playing with shadows and shooting from all angles. Neema had wanted someone who would provide more of a photojournalistic feel. She didn't discuss this with the photographer beforehand because she assumed she would love the photos since she was in awe of her friend's photos. Luckily, the photographers took around 1000 photos, so the couple had quite a few that they did in fact love.

Does your photographer and / or videographer shoot aerial photography/videography, or in transparent language, pictures and video from above? Some love capturing the full scene with a drone, especially if the landscape is spectacular, like a cityscape or beach.

Do you want more traditional photography with each person looking straight into the camera? Or would you prefer more candids where the photographer captures the emotions of the day without anyone being aware of them, in more of a photojournalistic style, capturing unexpected moments? You can have both!

*David Starke Photography*

You might want formal family photographs but then candids throughout the reception, skipping the traditional table pictures, which is very common these days. Or you might love the idea of having a photojournalistic feel with some direction from the photographer so the photos appear candid but are actually set up.

There are also fine art photographers who may have a softer approach with lighting and more of an angelic feel. Think "dreamlike," "heavenly," "romantic."

Others specialize in certain dramatic looks, with extreme contrast in lighting and/or details. For example, I work with one photographer who is known for his sunset evening shots because of the contrast in colors and shapes. I have also worked with another who captures the colors from the DJ lighting to really scream "dance party!" for the reception photos.

**_What do YOU want most when you see your photos? How do you want to FEEL?_**

If you're looking for a traditional and classic look, you might want to consider having the photographer shoot a mix of black and white as well as color images. You might also want some portrait shots. Ladies, between the strong emotions on the inside and the hair and makeup and dress on the outside, you're going to feel gorgeous, so I highly recommend some close-ups!

Remember, your photographer and videographer want to make you happy. If you love their style, which is why you or your Planner would've reached out to them, then letting them know what you hope to capture is completely understandable and very much appreciated by many photographers!

You can't redo that day, so 1) making sure you choose a photographer who shoots in a style you love and 2) making sure the photographer understands what you're looking for are both key elements to having photos you are excited about.

Personality is huge when it comes to photography too. I'm not saying that you need to adore them like you would your best friend. What I'm saying is that you need to feel at ease around them, a comfort level that allows you to be yourself and show your true emotions. Finding a photographer who gets your vibe and is a pleasure to work with before, during AND after your wedding day is very important. It's not just about the style of photography.

Telling each vendor what will make your special day the best day ever is really important. And if you're not sure (which is okay!), tell them what you DON'T like, so they understand you better.

Here are a few key points for you or your Planner to discuss with a photographer before the contract has been signed:

- What are the Package options offered?
- Is an Engagement Shoot included?
- How many photographers will be at the wedding? For the entire time?
- How many hours are included in the fee, and what is the additional cost for extra coverage?
- How many photos should I expect to receive as proofs? This is the number of photos they shoot that day. And how long do I have to wait before I am sent the proofs?
- How many should I expect to be edited?
- They will all be high resolution, correct?
- Are special effects extra? What type of special effects do you offer?

- Is retouching extra?
- What if I want photos taken at the brunch the next day, or at the rehearsal the night before? How do you charge for that?
- Is that the total price or do you have add-ons like a travel fee?
- What are my rights to the images? For example, if I want to make my own album or post digital proofs on social media, can I?
- Wedding Album Questions:
  - How many photos are included in an album?
  - Are the photos bleed (to the edges), or do they have a border?
  - Are there several photos to a page or one per page? What type of album options do you offer, and what are the prices?
  - How long does it take before I receive the first layout design?
  - How long does it then take to receive the album?

When you give them a list of shots you want to make sure they take that day, such as the "First Look" (if you're doing that), also let them know about special friendships and relationships you want to ensure they get as well.

**Side note:** Having a "First Look" means that you and your partner have decided that you will see each other in private prior to the ceremony. Many couples choose to have a "First Look" nowadays so they can have family photos taken before the ceremony instead of during cocktail hour as used to be the standard protocol.

For many couples I speak with, Video seems to be viewed as an extra rather than a necessary in the budget, but I can't tell you how much I value Cinematography for weddings.

While some still offer full videos, most summarize your day into a 3, 4, or 5 minute long video that you can watch on your phone or computer anytime you choose, whether that means you watch it when you're missing your partner or once a year on your anniversary. It's a way to reconnect without needing to do anything but watch for a few minutes and remember the stunning view from that day.

When I work with Cinematography partners, I tell them that I want to feel like I'm going to cry when I see the video. That's when I know it's ready to be sent to the client.

# THE DRESS

I can speak about suits and tuxes, but we all know that the dress, yes, THE dress, is just so much more fun to discuss! Sorry guys!

The number of options is so vast when it comes to wedding dress shopping, and although many of us would be giddy at the opportunity to buy one of every style, it's not often that we are awarded that opportunity. And so…we will have to make do with one or two. You guys, this is going to be FANTASTIC!

With a love for fashion since I saw my mother's statement necklace as I was rocked to sleep as an infant (haha), I go crazy over good bridal fashion!

*Ricky Restiano Photography*

I definitely suggest getting inspired by current styles by looking through magazines, websites and social media, but there are a few key recommendations I have when it comes to wedding dress shopping:

**1)  Have an open mind. This is truly key.**

A few years ago I took someone bridal dress shopping, and she was pretty adamant about what she knew she did not want – a ball gown. She absolutely did not want to purchase that style. Because we had a relationship and she trusted me, she knew that I was showing her dresses that were her style and that I thought she would love.

As soon as we entered the store and went upstairs, my eyes were drawn to this one dress. It sparkled, but not in an overt way. It had a shape that would make her body look svelte without being sultry. It was perfect.

I didn't say anything right away. We chose a few dresses together that she should try on, and then I asked her about trying that one, "Just try it." She agreed, and I'm sure you can guess the rest of the story. She looked absolutely gorgeous on her wedding day, and she wore a gown that looked nothing like she thought she would.

## 2) Think about your body type.

Don't think about the type of body you may want, or the body you think you have (Get the "Oh, I'm so fat" out! It's not doing you any good, so remove from your mindset!). What shape do you have? There is no good or bad. It's really about awareness so you can choose the most flattering style for your body.

What can be confusing to many is that different styles highlight different body parts, and while one person may say, "Oh, I don't want a Mermaid style because it shows off my big butt!" another may say, "Oh, I want a Mermaid style because it shows off my big butt!" What do you want to highlight that day?

And I'm not just talking about dresses. A huge trend is bridal suits, two piece dresses and bridal jumpsuits. Wear what makes you feel great!

*Christine Merson Photography*

### 3) Don't be afraid to shop around. It's your dress!

I remember wedding dress shopping for my own wedding years ago and being really upset when I found out that a dress I had loved in one store cost about 25% lower in another store. Thank goodness I hadn't bought the dress already! I didn't end up purchasing that dress at all, but I learned a lesson. Ask if it's their best price, and ask if the dress is exclusive to their store. Again, don't be afraid to ask questions.

### 4) Try on different shades of white and ivory, and try a pattern or color for some fun if you're into the idea!

It's craaaaazy how many various shades of white and ivory there are, so if you try on a dress and love the style but just aren't sure about the color, ask about color options and see fabric swatches!

The same color can appear different in various fabrics, so before deciding on a specific shade, make sure to see it in the fabric of the dress you're choosing. Satin has a sheen to it while lace is flat without embellishment added, tulle has a mesh-like feel, and silk shines as the light hits it. And thus, the same ivory color will appear unique on each.

One of the big trends for 2019 are black wedding gowns. Now, I don't see this as a trend that many will adhere to, but I do think those of you who want a unique statement-making look might love this idea. If you're going to go there, choosing a style that says, "bridal" is even more necessary if you want it to still say, "wedding dress." A black ball gown with a birdcage style veil just screams "avante garde" and "couture." Come on fashionistas, I can't wait to see you in this trend as well as some great prints! Floral wedding gowns are heavenly!

**5) From the inspiration you were attracted to, what element did all or many have?**

You may love clean lines or applique. You may be attracted to full gowns or one piece pantsuit options. Being aware of what you're attracted to will help you in being able to walk into the store and explain your likes and dislikes before trying on a few. The process of reviewing beforehand will help both you and the associate in streamlining the process and increase your chance of walking out with a look that you are in love with.

**6) If you think you want one type of sleeve, try the exact opposite as well.**

For example, you might be loving the regal long sleeve trend right now so you tell the associate at the bridal dress store that you definitely want long sleeve. Try on strapless too. I recommend this for two reasons:

1. After trying on several long sleeve options, you may feel like they are a little too similar and have a tough time noticing the differences, and

2.  Trying on extreme contrasts in sleeve styles allows you to really see whether you are loving the style you thought you would. Remember, not every style you see in a picture is going to be the style for YOU in the end.

If you're trying on all long sleeve dresses, you'll also want to try on a strapless dress just to cool down a bit!

I suggest trying on several shapes and sleeve styles. Sometimes we are shocked at what we end up loving. That story I was telling you about earlier, about the bride who ended up choosing the exact opposite style she thought she would, she chose strapless when she went in saying, "absolutely no strapless." What's 5 or 10 more minutes to just try it out?

7) **If you've decided to opt for 2 styles for your special day, that's a super fun idea! I recommend having the 2 looks be completely different.**

Decide from the start whether you're looking for both to be long, one to be long and one to be short, or one to be full and the other to be form-fitted. Or if you're planning on wearing a jumpsuit, really go for it for the reception! Are the shoes going to be different too? The change creates a bit of a dramatic entrance for the reception, so if there isn't a completely different look, I wouldn't recommend spending your hard-earned money on a second look. Hair and makeup can also be booked for 2 looks, many times to go with the 2 dresses, and with this I also recommend creating very different styles to really make a statement with each.

What else should I remember?

Also consider the number of hours you'll be standing, so I ALWAYS recommend bringing at least 2 pairs of shoes, one heel and one flat or one high heel and one lower heel, all dependent on the client, the dress and the setting of course. If you're getting married on a beach, no heels please! My point is that your feet will probably start hurting after a few hours, and the last thing you want is to be thinking about your feet or walking around like you are in pain.

Regarding suits and tuxes, the key elements are the fabric, the style, the cut, and the color. Remember, if you're going with a formal look, you want dark colors in a nice fabric. Really feeeeeel the fabric. Do you want a 2-tone, patterned or solid suit or tux? Most formal tuxes will be black with a white dress shirt and black bow tie, and don't forget the black shiny shoes!

If you're going the casual route in the warmer months or locations, have fun with linen in a khaki or olive green!

Wear what makes you feel like YOU and also makes your partner think, "Wow." That's the reaction you want, right?

*"Wow. I do not want to take my eyes off of you for one second you look so amazing."*

Creating "a look" is important for the partner who chooses to wear a suit or tux as well.

Tie or bow tie? Any patterns or just solid colors?

3 piece suit with a vest included?

Handkerchief in the pocket?

# HAIR AND MAKEUP

Many of my clients have found this part to be stressful. There is such a huge range when it comes to the financial investment you can make on hair and makeup. For example, you might have one offering to do your makeup for $250 and another for $650. Do you go with the least expensive if you like his or her work? Or do you go with the one who seems the busiest? Or the one who responds quickly to your emails?

Whether you decide on hair or makeup first, it doesn't matter as long as you narrow down your preferences to a few looks before your trials.

**Let's talk about hair first.**

What style dress did you choose? If it has a halter neck (around the neck), having an updo will elongate your neck and really show off the style of the dress.

Does your dress say glam? Go for a sultry style!

Does it say '70s hippie chic? Wear it in a romantic, loose style! Now, there are many variations to "romantic and loose," from updo styles to half up half down styles and all down, so these are general terms until you narrow down the styles you prefer.

Look at pictures in magazines (and not just bridal magazines) and social media for inspiration, as well as on TV (Award shows are the best for hair and makeup trends!). See what you like and if it goes well with your dress, and if you aren't sure, ask the stylist at your trial when you're discussing my next point as well.

What type of hair do you have?

If it's like mine and it gets frizzy easily (It's okay, I joke about it all the time!) and you're getting married in the heat of summer, you'll probably want it up or in a curled or wavy style (with lots of hairspray!), not just straightened (It won't end up looking straight!).

If you have short hair, do you want to wear it in the same style you usually do or do you want to style it differently that day? If you have naturally curly hair, do you want to wear it curly that day or go for a very different look and have it straightened or smoothed out and in an updo?

If you have fine hair, you might want to purchase high quality clip-in extensions or have extensions attached for your special day to get a look with more volume and / or length.

Once you have an idea of what you might want (I don't say "definitely want" because you probably won't know until you see what it looks like at your trial), you can view a stylist's past client photos to see their work, either on their social media or on their website. You'll probably notice right away that many stylists have a certain specialty. For example, let's say you want someone who is amazing at braids. You view one stylist's photos and they look beautiful! But no braids. That doesn't mean that they can't do braids well! Contact them, or have your Planner do so, to see if they have other examples of work they have done that they can send to you. If you have a Planner, he or she may also have a certain vision to go with your dress, and if you like it, they can help you in hiring someone to achieve that look.

### What about accessories?

There are some great stores that sell beautiful bridal hair accessories and jewelry, as well as veil options. I recommend trying on veils with the bridal accessories you plan on wearing so you can see what it will look like with something showing through the fabric.

Whether you decide on a Cathedral-length veil (very long and statement-making), a birdcage veil, or no veil at all, what you choose to accessorize with is very important. It can detract from your dress if it's too loud, or it can finish a look beautifully if done right. What goes best with your gown? Once you have that narrowed down, try on a few styles. I thought I would love the birdcage style, but when I tried it on I felt like I was wearing a costume! You just never know what you are going to feel your best wearing. I thought I would absolutely love that style, but it just didn't look right on me, or maybe I just didn't feel comfortable in that style in the end.

Whatever the reason, it wasn't the style for me. When you're trying on your wedding dress in the store, ask to try on a veil with it, and try to choose one that is at least similar to a style that is attractive to you. You'll get an idea of the length you prefer as well as the style, and if you feel comfortable in a veil at all. If you decide against wearing a veil, do you want to add a major hair accessory like a crown or jeweled headpiece? All ideas to consider.

Many jewelry options at these stores are statement pieces, so if you're looking for more of a classic look, I would ask you to consider having this be your "borrow" moment. That's the traditional in me peaking through!

*"Something borrowed, something new, something old and something blue."*

*Ricky Restiano Photography*

Does your grandmother have a pair of pearl earrings that would go perfectly with your dress? Having something sentimental with you while you walk down the aisle is really special, so it might be worth thinking about.

## Onto makeup!

You want the entire look to be like, "Yessss….that look is fire!" Thus, the hair and makeup really need to go together. You might love smoky, sultry makeup but then want a loose, beach-wave hairstyle to go with your flowing wedding dress, so just because you love a style doesn't mean it's the right style for that day. Even though I am a big proponent of, "It's your day, do what you want!" I also want you to be at your best and feel amazing, and that means creating a magical look that just WORKS.

Choosing a makeup professional who is truly an artist rather than someone who "just does makeup" will make a huge difference. Hiring someone who is up on the trends, who understands how to create a flawless (or close to it) face, who is pleasant before and during, and who listens to you are all very important points. Just like with the hairstylist, there are many makeup artists who have a specialty, whether creating a great highlight and contour, strong eyes, a "not too made up" look, or another in which they shine.

***What are YOU looking for?***

# WEATHER

It may be even more unpredictable in certain times of the year, but let's face it, the weather is just plain unpredictable.

I worked on an event a few months ago that was going to be entirely outdoors. We were all praying for good weather since the option to add a large tent needed to be decided several days in advance and for several thousand dollars outside of their budget. The true vision was to have the event outside, and thankfully the sun was shining the entire day. My clients wanted to take that chance, and it worked out for them. Consider the alternative if the event suddenly had to be brought indoors. For them, they were fine with bringing the guests inside and proceeding without all of the entertainment. But this is a personal decision that must be thought through when first booking the venue or location.

If your event is during the summer months, make sure to have lots of cold water available for your guests, as well as the option of personalized hand fans if you choose.

I'm currently working on a summer wedding that has all of the colorful floral summertime feels. We had the option of decorating the structure that's already set up for wedding ceremonies, but besides wanting to be different (Yes, of course!), I also became concerned about weather when I asked about the options if it rained. As in many cases, the venue staff just said, "We bring it inside." And that was that. But what about the beautiful greenery and the whole reason my clients chose to have the ceremony at that particular venue? After discussing several options with florists and explaining my vision to them (after my client confirmed loving it), we proceeded with an option that can be moved indoors if possible, allowing for a beautiful summer feel no matter what. We also continued the theme by creating centerpieces that brought the outside in. You just never know with weather, so having a backup plan, or creating décor that will work indoors as well, is highly recommended.

And what about winter weddings? A snowy background makes for gorgeous photography! So in some cases, you might actually WANT it to snow the day before your wedding so you have that wintery feel in your photographs. Just imagine the snow, the lights, the holiday décor all creating a gorgeous background for your photos.

Although we don't know what the weather will be like on a certain day, especially nowadays when it's 80 degrees in October, we can certainly consider the weather when deciding the overall style of your wedding.

Fall leaves, snowy grounds, fields of grass, gardens of blooming flowers, whatever makes your heart sing, the time of year is important when reviewing venues and possible dates for your wedding. Even if you do not have an outdoor ceremony and/or reception, the weather and time of the year will create a certain environment. But don't worry about rain! Didn't you ever hear that it's good luck? Some of the most magical photos of couples are when they have fun with the weather!

### See it:

*You're walking slowly, holding hands, each holding an umbrella in the opposite hand, staring at one another. Picture. You lean in for a kiss. Picture. The rain falling behind you and all around you. Gorgeous. The rain starts to slow down a bit. A rainbow forms. Picture.*

And that brings me to the point of this: Bring matching umbrellas.

# TRANSPORTATION

As we delve into transportation options, there are 3 areas to discuss:

1) Your transportation, 2) The transportation for your wedding party, and 3) The transportation for your out-of-town guests.

Let's go into the first point first (Yep, I said it.)

## 1) Your transportation

If you're not super into hiring a limo or fancy car for your wedding day, your first thought might be, "It's okay, I'll just drive."

And then it happens.

You are all ready and then you try to get into your car. Except you don't fit. And I don't mean YOU don't fit. I mean you in your dress or your dress alone won't fit. If you're wearing a form-fitted gown, you'll find it VERY difficult to slide into the driver's seat, or even passenger seat, and drive without feeling constricted and/or without your gown getting stuck near the gas or break (Emergency! Please, no!).

Okay, so driving is out. What about being in the passenger seat or even the backseat? It might work out, but it might not. Think about how little room cars have when you're wearing your everyday clothing. If your dress is a sheath or is made from a flowy fabric, it will probably work, but you just want to make sure before the big day. And you want to make sure the surroundings and the floor are extremely clean so nothing gets on your dress/outfit.

The only exception to driving yourself is if you are planning on getting dressed at the venue where both your ceremony and reception will be taking place. You'll be wearing your normal clothing on the way there, so why not?

If your ceremony is at one location, and then your reception is at another location, adding a vintage or sports car for the drive over can be a super fun addition for you and your spouse as long as you take the dress into consideration again.

Hiring a stretch limo allows for you to have an easier time getting in and out while wearing your dress. It also allows you to sit back and relax a bit before you say your vows and/or at the end of the reception when you're already completely relaxed!

<u>Depending on your wedding, you'll need a limo to be hired for:</u>

1. The hotel to the ceremony location, to the reception, and then back to the hotel (4 locations)

2. The hotel to the ceremony and reception location and then back to the hotel (3 locations)

3. The ceremony and reception location to the hotel at the end of the day/night (2 locations)

4.  The hotel to the ceremony location to the reception (3 locations)

or

5.  The hotel to the ceremony and reception location (2 locations)

The 4th and 5th options are for those of you who will be changing into a more comfortable clothing option for the reception, so you would either have a ride back to the hotel or after party, or you plan to ride on the shuttle bus you've organized for everyone else to transport back to the hotel.

## 2)  The transportation for your wedding party

What's your style and what tone do you want to set? If you want to set a tone of, "Let's party!" then book a Party Bus with lights, alcohol, and music for everyone to enjoy while being transported from the hotel to the wedding ceremony. If you want to set that tone, but after the ceremony when traveling to the reception (recommended!) and then later back to the hotel, that can be arranged as well.

You can also just have a hotel shuttle from the hotel to the ceremony, using the shuttle solely as a means of transportation.

Some people ask their wedding party to drive over to the ceremony, and if the reception is in another location, then drive over to the reception as well, providing a bus for them only at the end of the wedding when many have been intoxicated.

You know what I'm going to say by now, right? There is no wrong or right, just information that will hopefully allow you to make the best decision for YOUR wedding.

### 3) The transportation of your out-of-town guests

Depending on the formality of the wedding weekend, as well as the relationships you have to your guests, you have different options when it comes to setting up transportation for those traveling in for you from afar.

If you have many people coming from one city on a specific plane, I would recommend scheduling a private bus to pick them up from the airport and bring them to the hotel.

If everyone is coming from different places, don't make yourself crazy trying to schedule a pick up for everyone. I think it's a great idea to help them though. For instance, if you hear that one of your friends will be arriving at Laguardia Airport on Friday night and then you hear of another friend arriving that same night, putting them in touch to see if they would like to travel to the hotel together is allowing some pre-wedding friendships to form (which creates an even better dynamic at your wedding and possibly even future friendships for your friends!). And if you know that they have never been to NYC, it's not a bad idea to help them out further by providing them with travel options depending on where the hotel is located, such as a cab (to Manhattan), an Uber, or a shuttle to the hotel if the hotel provides one. It takes some prep work, but your friends and family traveling in will really appreciate it. And you love them, remember?!

For all formal affairs, I highly recommend having Valet service at the venue. Most of the more upscale venues will, but in case they don't, I would advise you to hire a private Valet service and make sure everyone is taken care of so guests don't feel like they need to open their wallets.

# FLOWERS

Choosing your flowers and floral décor can be one of the most fun parts about wedding planning if you allow it to be. It can also be one of the most trying parts. Flower options are extensive and the price ranges are vast. Working with a florist who understands your vision and is HAPPY to show and explain to you different possibilities is not always the easiest, but it is a necessary for ensuring you're both on the same page when it comes to expectations.

*It's very easy to let your guard down because you just don't understand the options (understandably!), but it's your wedding, and you deserve to be excited about every part of it!*

Do you have a certain flower that you've always envisioned being a part of your wedding?

Now, is that flower in season when you're planning on getting married?

*Ricky Restiano Photography*

I know, I know. I don't mean to be the bearer of bad news, so take that info and let out a deep breath. There are always answers! Whoop whoop!

Discussing the flowers you envision, or showing a visual of the style of your wedding, will allow the experts in their field to provide you with beautiful options. The amount of creativity great florists have is unimaginable, and I am in awe at their skill. Once you understand and agree on the type of flowers for your wedding, that word "trust" has to come into play. Release and allow...

When you view the venue, make sure to take note of the amount and type of flowers they have outside and inside. If you're planning on getting married at a different time of year then when you view the venue, ask what they usually display at the time of year when you plan to marry. Information is knowledge, and knowing that your venue always has yellow tulips inside and out will allow you to adjust your color scheme as well as modify the type of flowers you might purchase.

Below is a list of options you may want to discuss with the florist before receiving a full quote and signing a contract with them:

- Centerpieces
- Escort Card Table
- Welcome Area
- Cocktail Tables
- Cake Table
- Chuppah, Archway, or non -traditional area where you will be stating your vows
- Ceremony walkway
- Bridal Bouquet
- Mother of the bride
- Mother of the groom
- (Don't forget the step parents if they are involved!)
- Grandparents on both sides
- Flower Girl
- Bridesmaids
- Maid / Maitron of Honor
- Ring Bearer
- Groomsmen
- Best Man

Many of you are also changing things up a bit from the traditional "sides," so be open with the florist about this from the start. For example, if you're not having traditional "bridesmaids," but you do want flowers for your best friend to walk down the aisle, let them know so they can include that in the quote.

Also consider your guests when deciding on your centerpieces. The worst is when your guests can't see each other because of the flowers.

I will also tell you a personal story that happened many years ago that enters my mind every time I discuss centerpieces with clients.

I was attending a formal wedding, wearing a black gown. I felt beautiful and the night was lovely.

And then it happened.

I leaned over to get something on the table and one of the centerpiece candles melted wax onto my gown. Now, I'm glad the flame didn't catch (grateful!), so that's number one, but I was so upset that my dress suddenly had wax all over it that I rushed into the bathroom to try and get it off, and about an hour later, I came out with most of it scraped off, but feeling flustered.

When placing candles on the tables, consider your guests' reach. In the story above, the candles dripped down on me, but whether high or low, just consider the implications of having candles as a part of your centerpiece. The effect of viewing tables with candles around or in the centerpieces can be gorgeous though, so it's just thinking about the HOW and the WHAT.

# MUSIC

---

Do you love the '80s'? Or Oldies? Current pop music?
Or heavy metal?

Now write that down. Write down your favorite style of music.

Now write down any style of music you just cannot STAND, if any.

The music you can't stand is out of the question. It is not going to be
played at your wedding.

With regard to your favorite style of music, what are your favorite
songs in that style? Sit down together and write down 10.

Now go through that list and determine the good songs to dance to.

If none of them are, keep those songs under an "Other" list for now.
If most of them are good dance songs, list them as such.

Now think of songs that MAKE you want to dance. You
don't have to actually like dancing to know which songs make

people want to dance, songs that have a good beat. Think, "Michael Jackson" songs, "Justin Timberlake" songs, and others.

Sometimes a couple doesn't like dancing so they decide they don't want any dance music, but the energy increases when there is some upbeat music played at a wedding, so I would advise you to have an open mind.

In the end, you'll have a list of songs that are 1) good to dance to, and a list of songs that are 2) some of your favs but are softer or not dance-type music (like heavy metal).

Now, if heavy metal is your favorite, think of your guests and whether they would enjoy that music as well. If you don't think any of them would, keep that for your music you enjoy on your way to the wedding, for your alone time. If you think they would enjoy it, add it to the list!

Let's say you love classical music, but you want to make sure you have an upbeat, crazy dance party kind of wedding. Why not hire a harpist or violinist to play during dinner or during your cocktail hour and a DJ or band for the reception?

Will you want to have a first dance together? If you do, will you want to take any professional dance classes together beforehand or just wing it and enjoy yourselves? What about Mother/Son, Father/Daughter dances? Traditional religious dances?

My husband and I decided to surprise everyone with a unique first dance. We started out lip syncing to a self-choreographed dance to each other and then started dancing together. It was such a fun experience for the two of us, and it added a bit of entertainment for the guests.

*Ricky Restiano Photography*

When you are deciding on the WHO you want to entertain your guests, watch videos of them in action, listen to stories from people, hear their voice over the phone if they are going to be the MC. It's also a good idea to find out if the person you are speaking to is the one who is actually going to be the MC at your wedding. I have seen situations where the bride thought they were having one person come and another worked the event.

What kind of atmosphere and personality do you want at your wedding? Someone who will get people on the dance floor or someone who will be in the background and only speak in order to let guests know when speeches are going to get started?

If you do want specific people giving speeches, make sure to ask them in advance so they feel well prepared and more at ease. Imagine someone asking you that day to come up with a speech for their big day? No thanks! Nerves, nerves! So ask them at least a few weeks in advance. You might want to have the traditional names be called up to make a speech, parents, Maid / Maitron of Honor, Best Man, but you may also want to give someone else the honor as well. If you aren't having a wedding party, choose a couple of people to say something meaningful (and possibly humorous if you'd like).

I like to speak to my clients in advance and find out if they want me to give the DJ or band a cue if the speeches are going on too long, and most do, but I would recommend asking the honorees if they'd like to prepare a speech by saying something like this:

"We would be so honored if you would prepare a 4 or 5 minute speech for our wedding since you know both of us well and would be so entertaining for everyone."

DJ's also often offer lighting options, as well as photo booth varieties for your guests to enjoy throughout the day or evening. I have to tell you, it never gets old. While the actual styles of the booth modernize, the fact that people love taking pictures and sharing them (especially now on social media) does not change. Whether you choose a style that the DJ offers or you opt for a vendor who works separately, adding a photo booth to a wedding is an easy way to add a piece of extra entertainment.

## EXTRA ENTERTAINMENT

If you really want to surprise your guests with a fun extra piece of reception entertainment, there are endless options ranging from fire dancers to on-the-scene painters. It really just depends on how elaborate you want to get!

I would advise considering the type of scene you want and keeping that in mind even when discussing the entertainment. You might get caught up in the idea of having clowns on stilts and then realize that the idea SO does not go with your formal affair. Or you love animals so you decide to have a petting zoo since you're having an outdoor backyard wedding, but then you realize that you may end up smelling like some of the animals and that is really not a sexy look for after the wedding. I love unique wedding ideas, so I'm not against any of these (You can shower after your wedding and get the smell off – it's okay!).

*Whatever will allow you and your guests to have a wonderful experience is the right answer.*

# MENU PLANNING

Most formal affairs will have a printed menu for guests to review and place their order when the servers request their choice.

I love a good printed menu that matches the entire theme. For instance, let's say your wedding is going to have tons of greenery around, having a menu with a leaf pattern will add to the continuity. You can also match your menu design to your invitation.

When you're asking guests to dress the part, you need to make sure they are treated the part as well. They walk in, they feel amazing, and then they are told there is a buffet where they can go up and grab some food. Ummm…I don't think they would be too happy.

However, if you tell guests it's a casual affair and then they see that there is a buffet, that's expected and you'll get a totally different reaction! It's all about expectation and then meeting or exceeding those expectations. Hmmm…life goals!

Just like the Music, you want to make sure you have enough variety for all different tastes.

Let's say you love Mexican food. You decide you want a taco station, a burrito station, a meat carving station with Mexican spices and flavors, and other complementary dishes during cocktail hour. That sounds amaaaaazing, right?!

But wait, doesn't your dad hate Mexican food? And suddenly you are not quite sure who likes or doesn't like Mexican food!

Okay, okay, it's going to be totally fine. Why don't you have a Mexican station? Add a little flair into your American food cocktail hour. Or have each station be completely different! For example, you might have a Mexican station with mini burritos, an Indian station with chana tikka masala and basmati rice, an American station with mini sliders and lobster rolls, and a Thai station with plates of pad thai and spring rolls.

There are several options for the entrée as well.

If you're having a formal style, it's customary to have a meat, a chicken and a fish entrée, as well as a vegetarian option. If the venue or caterer is charging you a hefty penny for the food, request a vegetarian option that incorporates unique touches, such as Vegetarian Lasagna made with ricotta cheese made from almonds, or a beautiful arrangement of 4 different colorful dishes on one plate. The expected couscous or pasta with is just too ordinary for a formal affair.

With a buffet, you want to stick with one type of ethnicity regarding entrée choice since guests will be adding several to their plates. You don't want a dish with tomatoes to be paired with a creamy dish, as that won't sit right with many stomachs, so consider that as well. I advise making sure there is at least one vegetarian option AND one vegan option. To explain further, if you have one meat, one chicken and one vegetarian pasta dish, you aren't leaving the vegetarians, vegans, gluten-free or lactose intolerant with many options. So yes, some people add a salad in there, but seeing guests eat a salad for their main entrée is a pretty disappointing site.

The increasing-in-popularity food trucks and pizza delivery stations are a fun way for a casual wedding to allow for a no-pressure, light atmosphere. Some couples are booking these trucks for their backyard weddings while others are booking them to provide extra food post wedding.

Some venues and caterers also offer the option to add an ice cream bar, a donut station, a fresh fruit station and other dessert in addition to the cake. It is very common nowadays to have many choices of dessert.

I've only seen one wedding where the couple did not want to have a cake, and they had cupcakes out instead. Guests were a little confused of whether there would be a cake since nothing was mentioned. I would say that if you're going to have cupcakes instead, present them in a way that makes them a focal point as the cake would be. For example, you might want to have the cupcakes added to a few tiers with a large cupcake on the top along with a flower or cake topper.

When people are eating well, they are generally happy and able to enjoy the other festivities and entertainment as well. And when the food is good, they will tell you many times over. Watch…at the brunch the next morning…you'll hear about the food from the day/night before!

I am also a big proponent of open bars at weddings (and this is coming from someone who rarely drinks alcohol). Since most couples opt for an open bar, unfortunately it seems "cheap" if a couple does not nowadays. I'm sorry, I said it, but I speak honestly and openly, and when people are expected to bring cash to a wedding, you are bound to hear mumbles and grumbles. Top notch venues will include an open bar automatically, but if you're having separate catering or your wedding at a less opulent venue, I would suggest considering this.

If you don't want a full open bar, you can include certain drinks, giving guests the option to pay for others that they specifically want, and that is widely acceptable as well. For example, you might choose to have name brand alcohol rather than the least expensive "house" brand, a specialty drink (more about that in a minute), and 2 types of wine, again not "house" brands.

If you truly cannot afford to include anything but the basics, I would suggest making it clear with a formal sign stating the options. Having the options listed out on a nice sign will elevate the formality. Without that, you can imagine guests asking for a certain drink, being told that they don't have it, asking for another and being told once again that they don't have it, and so on and so on.

If you do have alcohol at your wedding, especially an open bar, keep in mind that some people handle alcohol better than others. And so, if you don't want certain people being able to get up and give a speech at a moment's notice, let your Planner know in advance so he or she speaks to the venue and/or music entertainment about keeping the speeches limited.

Specialty drinks are a super fun addition for the couple as well as the guests. You can go the full "Bennifer" or "Brangelina" route, combining names for your drink name, or create a cute name that means something to the two of you. Let's say you both love dancing ballroom and you want to incorporate that into your wedding somehow without performing a tango dance, having a specialty drink called the, "Mango Tango" is a cute way of adding in a more intimate detail to the wedding reception.

If you would like a non-alcoholic wedding, still consider a specialty drink, just without added alcohol to it. You can have "mocktails," with additions such as mint or lychee! Just because you don't want alcohol present doesn't mean the drink options have to be limited to soda and/or juice. Creative drinks are an awesome way to add some spunk to the party! And that's with or without alcohol.

Whether you include alcohol or not, speaking to the caterer or the venue about the bartending staff is also a subject rarely spoken about. How many bartenders will be working (very important question since the last thing you want is everyone standing around the bar waiting for a drink)? Do you want drink specialists who can create creative drinks, or are you satisfied with the standard, "Yes, I can certainly pour you a glass of the Chianti?" Does it sound amazing to have bartending staff who can throw drinks or create lavish works of art, or is your first reaction, "Who cares?" If drinks are a big part of your wedding, these are questions to discuss with your venue and /or caterer.

# CAKE

Wedding cake prices range enormously in price, so before you even take a look at cake designs, decide what the design and taste of a cake is worth to you. Is it one of your major must have moments to have a lavish cake or is it just an extra at your wedding?

Most bakers are going to ask you,
*"Do you want Fondant or Buttercream frosting?"*

And you will look at them with wide eyes and a shrug that says,
*"Whichever tastes good?"*

So let's go through the options:

Fondant allows for more intricate design and a smooth finish with a harder feel. If you are looking for stripes, balls, realistic looking flowers, or other details to be added to your cake, you'll most likely want fondant. But definitely check with the specific baker because it also depends on their expertise! Fondant is the pricier of the two options, so do keep that in mind if you are looking for a budget-friendly cake. Buttercream is a less expensive option, but it's the perfect choice for a rustic feel or for hand-piped flower roses.

Think outside of the box! You can have an ombre airbrushed cake with bright colors if you like! Or you can have a simple white cake with fresh flowers added on top!

You can even have a cake in the shape of items from your theme! For example, let's go back to the Halloween theme example. The two of you met at a Halloween party, so you'll be getting married in October and are super excited to incorporate your theme into every part of your wedding. A 3 tier cake might be fun, each layer a different shade of deep red or plum for a bit of a gothic style. Or you might prefer a cake that looks like a large box with a few different costumes coming out of it, from Wonderwoman to a Ghost to an Angel, all made from Fondant for a more literal iteration.

### *The options are endless.*

Regarding flavors, that's what you decide at your tasting. You want to choose flavors you both love of course, but it's respectful to also consider what you think most people would enjoy. Do you want a really unique flavor like Chocolate Chunk Red Velvet, or would you prefer to offer a flavor or two you think most would like, such as the standard Chocolate or Vanilla? I highly recommend bringing a couple of people to the tasting, if the bakery allows, since you may love 5 flavors and be unsure of which to choose! Not a bad problem to have (wink wink).

*Christine Merson Photography*

If you are Vegan, Gluten-Free and / or Dairy-Free, I SUPER highly recommend (the highest of the high) viewing and tasting the bakery's cake before your wedding. Many bakeries now offer gluten-free, but they are dry and /or tasteless. Not as many offer dairy-free, but when they do, some are so sweet that they are barely edible, and others lack the creaminess. There are great bakeries out there who make amazing cakes, so it's just about taste-testing beforehand. It's not just about who says, "Sure! We can do that!" but about those who say they can and show examples beforehand.

When working with a venue, many times a "standard venue cake" is included. Make sure to get more information on what that means. What is "standard?" You or your Planner can contact the bakery or bakery options to find out more about their standard cakes. Many times, the bakeries provide examples on their website for both your and their convenience. Often, I view the standard and ask about a few other ideas so I can provide my clients with options on the style / design.

# MONEY

---

**The dreaded topic of money.**

No matter what your budget, I have not found money to be anyone's favorite subject. I want you to be prepared rather than shocked.

For the first few months of wedding planning, you may feel like all of your hard-earned money is very quickly being dispersed. And that can feel a bit scary. I'm here to say that after those few months you will feel better and more in control again.

Think about the major bookings that occur in the first few months of wedding planning:
Your ceremony and reception location(s)
Photographer
Videographer
Dress(es)
Wedding Planner
Florist
Musical Entertainment
Possibly extra entertainment
Hair and Makeup

There are others that may be included for your specific wedding, but the above is the general list for many of you. After those have been booked, you will have other expenses, but you will feel less like money is draining out of your pockets. Wedding costs can definitely add up, but it is the day that you are going to remember forever, and you want it to be amazing. I totally get it, and you have to work with people who "get it."

There are some businesses out there that try to take advantage and raise their prices for weddings because they know they can, so you want to feel good about who you hire.

"Do I feel the quality of service or product matches the quote they are providing? Do I feel comfortable?"

*If you aren't comfortable with the amount from the start, you may become resentful and your relationship with that business will suffer. You want a beautiful dynamic at your wedding, so surround yourself with those who make you feel happy, gorgeous, stress-free and excited.*

Whatever your total budget, and that's not for me to provide to you because I don't know your personal financial situation, take that total and break it apart. Unless you are going to have the reception at a private home, the venue will utilize a large portion of the budget. Decide the other areas that are super important to the two of you, whether that's making sure you have an amazing photographer and beauty team or great music to dance to and someone to plan the entire day for you, which are the areas that deserve the larger ratio of your budget?

When it comes to tipping, there are so many articles out there with different thoughts on who to tip as well as the amount to tip. Just like the restaurant industry, the Event Planning industry is a service industry. That means that most people who work in the industry count on tips, and if you think someone went above and beyond, tipping is greatly appreciated. Whether it's the flower delivery guy or the hairstylist, whether it's the assistant or the owner, everyone contributing service to your wedding should be "counted" when budgeting your tips closer to the wedding date.

What I advise my clients to do is to label envelopes with every business name associated with your special day. Then write out on a piece of paper what you think each should receive with regard to tip money. Add that amount into each envelope. DO NOT SEAL IT. Make one more envelope with extra cash inside. On your wedding day, you will either have your Wedding Planner or someone else whom you can trust to hand out the envelopes to the vendors while you enjoy your day. Before any envelopes are provided though, depending on the service that day, you may want to add additional cash from the "Extra" envelope. If any balances are due that day, I would advise creating separate envelopes for the balances so the service providers clearly see that they are being paid the balance as well as an additional tip.

Writing a great online review is also a wonderful way to add an extra "thank you" if you thought the service was fantastic. The wedding industry counts on reviews in a huge way now, so leaving a positive review after your wedding is very much appreciated by all.

## BUDGET-STRETCHING TIPS

A big misconception is that hiring a Wedding Planner is very expensive. I recently had a client so thrilled that within a week or two of working together, I had already saved her more money than she had spent on my services in total. Literally, by them hiring me they SAVED money. I can't say that about every Planner out there, but I can say that hiring someone who is skilled in negotiation and relationship building will definitely save you money. It sounds kind of nuts that you have to spend some money to save money, but if you hire the right person/people, it works!

Another way to save money is to keep your eyes open for promotions, as I had discussed earlier in the Invitations portion of this book. With regard to accessories, shoes, jewelry, even the dress (Hello…trunk shows!), there are many opportunities to purchase or rent items at a lower cost.

# IMPORTANT EXTRAS

# WELLNESS

---

### "Eating healthy for your wedding."

Now what did most of you hear me say when you read that?

Did you hear,
"Okay, this is how I can lose weight for my wedding day"

Or did you hear,
"Great, I definitely want to feel energized, renewed and great on the inside and outside!"

When you commit to eating healthier foods, you are committing to your body, inside and out. You are committing to becoming your best self by feeding your mind and body what it truly craves (not the sugar talking), to eating when it wants food, to supplying it with nutrients that make you feel sharp, strong, and clean. I added the "for your wedding" to make a point, but when I work with clients on eating healthier for their wedding, I am also helping them create new habits so they continue post wedding as well.

There is a common desire to look the best you've ever looked in your life on your wedding day, so brides-to-be diet and get as skinny as they can for the wedding day, and then after the wedding some gain the weight back. And then do you know what happens? Many people look at their wedding photos and, unfortunately, immediately see their body and how different they looked. That creates a cycle of feeling disappointed with themselves and back on the diet rollercoaster.

I have never believed in "diets." Diets mean you restrict your body from certain foods and then eat them again once you're "off the diet." When you are "allowed" to eat them again because you aren't on the diet, you are most likely overeating as well since you had restricted yourself. That ruins your metabolism and creates a mentality that you did something "bad."

*Smiling Through Chaos Tomato Soup and Grilled Cheese*

I believe in healthy eating. I believe in eating what works for your specific body and no one else's.

For my entire life, I have heard this statement, "Olive oil is good for you." But olive oil is BAD for me. I feel sick from olive oil. So should I eat it because everyone says it's good for you? That's how I approach every single situation when it comes to health and wellness.

So I'm not going to write a list of foods that are "good for you" or "bad for you" because I don't know YOU yet (www.SmilingThroughChaos.com to change that!).

I WILL advise you to eat a food and then analyze whether it made you feel great, okay, or not so good. For example, I remember trying kale for the first time several years ago, and I felt super energized afterwards! THAT is a good food for my body. On the opposite spectrum, if I eat Chinese food (which I do sometimes!), I never feel great. I don't feel sick; I just don't feel greeeaaaattt…. Know what I mean?

And there are certain foods that just aren't good for anyone, like sugar.

This includes foods that have a high natural sugar content too, like corn. Not to give corn a bad rap but it has barely any nutritional value. So enjoy it every once in awhile, but it shouldn't be in your daily consumption. Peas are like corn, as are snap peas.

Actual sugar makes the body feel energized and giddy and then crash, so again, this is not a diet, so I'm not going to say "never," but keep it to a minimum. I will, however, advise you to eat the real thing rather than adding artificial sweeteners to your coffee or into your baked goods.

And about those baked goods. I'm all about them! It's just about using nutritious ingredients that keep you satisfied with the taste and how full the food keeps you. Are you hungry an hour later? You might not be eating enough protein. Are you feeling lightheaded? You might not be eating enough calories or enough grains.

Over 15 years ago (Ugh, I'm aging myself right now), when I was studying abroad in England. I had a tough time finding food that I could eat since I have a few food intolerances and allergies. There are probably more options there now, but back then, if you were gluten free that meant you didn't eat bread unless you wanted to suffer through the bread that crumbled as soon as you picked it up (fun times). While I was living there, I found that I was a little lightheaded after the first few weeks. Upon review of my daily diet, I realized that I was not eating enough grains for my body. As soon as I started making sure to add more grains in, I felt better.

Point proven that "low carb" isn't "good for everyone."

Some people feel great with a high fat diet while others feel lethargic eating the same foods.

**Each of our bodies are different, so why wouldn't the food we need to fuel them be as well?**

This is your unique story, your unique body, and your unique feeling. Pay attention to what makes you feel good, and if you would like more of a personalized approach, discuss options with an expert for a holistic approach to food and achieving your health and wellness goals (not a diet).

And what about when you eat out? Or should you make sure you don't eat out at all for the final few months before you get married? Those are the questions that go through people's minds, and rightfully so when you want to look and feel your best for the most amazing day, right? So here's my answer:

### *Create a mindset of balance.*

When I say "balance," I mean mentally, spiritually, physically and emotionally. I already generally spoke about balance in the food world, as in carbs to protein to fats, but I mean be kind to your body.

When you're hungry, eat foods that make you feel energized, refreshed and healthy!

Be mindful when you're eating and stop when you feel satisfied.

Try to eat at home as often as possible, and when you eat out, choose the foods that will make you feel good. You might not know these right away, and that's okay if there is trial and error. That's life, and that's how we learn! When I discuss restaurant food with my clients, I first listen to what they usually order, and then I make modifications to those before I offer suggestions of other meal ideas as well.

### *It's not about creating a life of restriction; it's about creating a life of fulfillment.*

Take a few minutes a day to review how you are feeling, your energy levels, your mood, your stress and anxiety levels, your physical ailments (or not), your ability to relax (or not), and your level of excitement for the little moments in life.

*Can you just imagine your wedding day, feeling so clear-headed, vivacious, confident and happy?! Food is medicine to so many parts of us, internally and externally.*

While I was studying at the Integrative Institute for Nutrition (IIN) (I still can't believe that I had the immense honor), I was able to see and hear the founders of just about every diet out there stand in front of me on stage and speak about the diets. As the Founder of IIN told us, after every lecture, we would start to believe that THAT diet was the best diet. In the end, and I think this was his point the entire time, we had to find the right combination for ourselves and for others. It's not about following one diet, it's about learning about the positives and negatives of each and applying the best method for each individual body.

A big part of my schooling at IIN was also realizing, through watching many role plays on stage, that the way someone eats almost always comes back to something else occurring in their lives. And when I think back to the different times of my life, when I've lived through major life challenges, I did eat differently through many of them, not all, but many.

If you're super happy, loving your career, feeling like you have lots of friends and a great home life, you're in love and they're in love with you too (wink wink), and you're excited for the future, you're most likely not coming home to delve into a large bag of chips without any dinner and then go to bed. It CAN happen! I'm definitely not saying it can't, I'm saying it's not as likely. When you feel good, you want to continue feeling good, and a bag of chips won't help you to feel energized, quick, clear in mind and skin, and ready to achieve all of your goals.

So while you think about what you want for your wedding day, you probably imagine feeling amazing. The hair and makeup and dress can help you feel that way, but it starts before that. It starts by feeling relaxed through yoga and energy balancing, strong from exercise and healthy eating, and by truly loving yourself.

<u>Here's a favorite recipe of mine.</u>
I like to use a mini pancake pan to make mini pancakes and enjoy a small stack!

## Smiling Through Chaos Protein Pancakes

<u>Ingredients:</u>
Birch Benders gluten-free pancake and waffle mix
1 scoop Pure bone broth powder (chocolate or original
1 scoop collagen powder
1-2 tsp Navitas goji powder
1 banana sliced – optional
Enjoy Life dairy-free chocolate chips and Sunfood cacao nibs mixed together – optional
Spectrum Coconut Oil spray

<u>Directions:</u>
Pour 1.5 cups Birch Benders mix into large bowl.
Add 1.3 cups water into bowl.
Add bone broth, collagen and goji powder in.
Mix all together and let sit for 1 minute while stovetop heats pan pre-sprayed with Spectrum coconut oil spray.
Spoon pancake mix onto pan and add optional items.
Heat on medium low (or higher if you like them more burnt) until starting to bubble.
Flip and let heat 1-2 more minutes.
Enjoy warm!

Try adding foods into this spreadsheet as you take notice about your food intake:

| FOODS THAT MAKE ME FEEL GREAT! | FOODS THAT MAKE ME FEEL HORRIBLE | FOODS THAT DON'T SEEM TO AFFECT ME SO MUCH |
|---|---|---|
| | | |
| | | |
| | | |
| | | |
| | | |
| | | |
| | | |
| | | |
| | | |

# THE MEANING OF IT ALL

What are you doing all of this for?

You will remember that moment, the moment you stare into each other's eyes while making the commitment to each other in front of your friends and family. You will remember the feeling of having your loved ones around you while dancing up a storm.

So again, why are you doing all of THIS?

If everything you'll remember most will be about the feeling, what is all the planning for?

When you have a wedding ceremony and reception that has been well thought out and planned, everything else comes together so smoothly and you're able to focus on just enjoying yourselves. When you feel your most beautiful / handsome, when you are enjoying the food and the drinks, when you have your special dances, and all the other amazing moments of that day, you will know why you did it all.

*Throughout this process, it can seem like A LOT at times, and it may feel overwhelming, but if you work with the right team of professionals and keep your focus on creating a beautiful environment for the two of you to start your lives together, it will be magic.*

Cheers to YOU. Cheers to making it amazing and starting off your marriage with a great big bang of smiles and happiness.

# VENDOR

| Contact Name | Phone Number | Email Address | Social Media @ |
|---|---|---|---|
|  |  |  |  |
|  |  |  |  |
|  |  |  |  |
|  |  |  |  |
|  |  |  |  |
|  |  |  |  |
|  |  |  |  |
|  |  |  |  |
|  |  |  |  |

# MANAGEMENT (CONTINUED)

| Deposit Amount | Deposit Date | Balance Due | Balance Due Date |
|---|---|---|---|
|  |  |  |  |
|  |  |  |  |
|  |  |  |  |
|  |  |  |  |
|  |  |  |  |
|  |  |  |  |
|  |  |  |  |
|  |  |  |  |
|  |  |  |  |

# NOTES

_____

_____

_____

_____

_____

_____

_____

_____

_____

_____

_____

_____

_____

_____

_____

_____

_____

_____

_____

# ABOUT AMANDA HUDES

*Amanda Hudes is the Founder of Smiling Through Chaos event planning. Through her business, Amanda helps to relieve busy women from the stress that can come along with coordinating weddings and other major lifetime events. She also helps them to look and feel their best in the process. Smiling Through Chaos offers everything needed for an amazing event.*

*Amanda Hudes received a B.S. with honors in Advertising Marketing Communications from the Fashion Institute of Technology in NYC. During and after her time at F.I.T, Amanda* worked with world-renowned fashion designers and in the corporate marketing and product development sectors of fashion and beauty for major brands.

Amanda grew up with food intolerances, so during her time at F.I.T., Amanda realized that she did not have to make ONE choice in her career and decided to start a meal planning business (the A+ Plan) when word-of-mouth of her dietary knowledge and ability to help women lose weight quickly in a healthy way became so great. A few years later, she attended and graduated from the Integrative School for Nutrition (IIN) as a certified Health Counselor, gaining knowledge from the founders of every major diet out there. Throughout the years since, she has helped all ages in feeling and looking their best through healthy, mindful eating. She later became certified in Yoga, Barre, Group Fitness and Sports Conditioning, and Reiki.

Amanda moved out of the corporate fashion world and into a corporate management role, supervising and managing teams and multiple projects occurring simultaneously, planning all events, and creating warm and inviting environments. It was then that Amanda realized she, unlike many, did not get stressed when planning events, and that she could use her expertise and experience to help other busy women plan their events and help them look and feel their best in the process. Combining the A+ Plan with her event planning and management experience, she created "Smiling Through Chaos," focusing on helping clients smile through it all. Years later, Amanda is excited to continue her work in the event world while sharing her experience and expertise with others.

**Visit www.SmilingThroughChaos.com**

Made in the USA
Monee, IL
12 May 2022

96313161R00074